Anger Management

How To Get Rid Of Anxiety And Prevent It From Ruining Your Relationship With Your Child Before It's Too Late To Do Anything About It

(Learn How To Keep Your Feelings And Emotions Under Control In Order To Calmly Resolve Tantrums)

Elton Burton

TABLE OF CONTENT

Be Dedicated To The Task At Hand 1
Having A Good Handle On Your Angry Feelings 6
Our Tempers Are Quick To Flare By Nature. 13
Issues Of A Physcial Nature That Result From Being Angry 18
When It Comes Down To It, There Is Just One Approach That Will Work For Anger Management. 24
How To Handle Angry Feelings 27
Putting Your Mindfulness Into Practice 30
How To Control Your Angry Emotions 39
Keep A Record Of Your Wrath In A Diary. 50
Dangerous Obstacles 57
Dealing With The Physical Effects Of Angry, Stressful, And Anxious Thoughts And Feelings 65
Do You Think You Owe It? Here Are Some Tips To Help You Get Over The Guilt You Feel After Losing Your Cool With Your Children. 70
Home-Based Work Involving The Use Of Triggers 76
Keeping Control Of Our Angry Moods And Our Children 85
Causes Damage To Relationships 97
Reduce Everything To Nothing 102

- The Influence Of Making An Apology 113
- Adjusting Your Personal Triggers 125
- The Languages Of Apology 135
- Maintaining The Barest Minimum Of Temper Tantrums 141
- A Guide To Be Used By Parents 146
- Causes And Reasons For Anger 156
- The Roots And Origins Of Angry Feelings 166

Be Dedicated To The Task At Hand

Therapists and other behavioral specialists agree that the most efficient method to change a specific habit or improve a deficiency is to first establish the desire to do so, and then to make a firm commitment to following through with that goal. If you want to be able to control your anger, the first step you need to do is to develop a strong emotional connection to this objective. This may happen when you give some serious thought to the unpleasant ways in which your anger problems are harming your life.

Close your eyes for a second and reflect on the state of your life as it is right now. Consider the relationship issues you are experiencing, the fact that you are unable to concentrate on your work, the fact that you continue to argue with loved ones, the fact that you continue to brood over a single upsetting event and complain about it, the fact that you are unable to look out for your own well-being, let alone the well-being of your children, and the fact that nothing in your life makes any sense. Connect it to the anger you have suppressed, which is now building up inside you, or to the fact that you lash out at others, and how this irritates you to the core despite the fact that you feel powerless to change it.

Now, think about how much better things would be if you were able to develop better anger management skills. Think about how little disagreements would never escalate into full-blown conflicts; how you would no longer feel lightheaded and emotionally spent all the time; how you would be able to focus more intently on your job; and how you would cease exaggerating the significance of seemingly insignificant issues.

Think about how much more level-headed, cool, and collected you will become, as well as the great impact this will have on your self-assurance, happiness, and general well-being. Think about how much more time you would have if you didn't waste it fighting about pointless matters; you could use that time into pursuing your goals instead of petty disagreements. Consider the calm and serenity that will one day replace the emotional upheaval that is now suffocating you, and you will discover that your life once again has a sense of purpose.

Write down your reflections on this topic, and then utilize the reasons you've given to drive you to concentrate on reining in your explosive temper. First, you need to acknowledge that you have an issue with managing your anger, and then you can go on to setting a goal based on that. You may say something like, "I have issues with anger management, and I am going to work on this and improve." as an example.

The next step is to consider when you would want to begin working toward the goal, what it is that you hope to achieve, and the reasons why you want to work toward the objective. For instance, your statement of purpose may go as follows: "Starting August 1st, I will work on finding healthier ways to manage my anger so that I can manifest a life that is joyful, peaceful, and prosperous with my family." This makes it very apparent why you want to address your problems: so that you may have a happy life with your family. Furthermore, the fact that you want to start working on it on August 1 makes it crystal plain when you need to finally stop putting things off.

After you have finished going through this stage, make it a point to read over your mission statement many times throughout the day. This will help you to keep your dedication front and center while you work with fervor toward achieving your goal.

After that, you will need to make use of a variety of techniques for anger management that will assist you in progressively reducing the issue, enhancing your sense of self-awareness, growing your emotional intelligence, and gaining greater self-control and mastery of your anger.

Having A Good Handle On Your Angry Feelings

Now that you have a slightly better sense of what anger is all about, you can clearly see why you may have had difficulty confronting the matter front on. Now that you have a somewhat clearer idea of what anger is all about, you can see why you may have had difficulty doing so. In point of fact, since anger management is so hard, a whole business has been built up around the concept of addressing it in the most effective manner possible. This is not to mean, however, that the only way to bring your anger under control is in a professional environment, since it is possible for you to perform just as well, if not even better, with a tailored anger management plan that you construct on your own. A much like anger itself, the correct strategy is going to be different for everyone, and the only way you can know whether you are on the right road is if you give it a try. A lot like anger itself, the right plan is going to be different for everyone.

Programs for the control of anger

People who struggle with anger problems may benefit greatly from participating in anger management programs since these programs often give extremely specific healing instructions. More significantly, though, it gives people who want to pursue this way with a controlled area in which they may express their feelings without having to worry about relapsing into habits that are less helpful. In addition to this, it offers individuals productive outlets for their anger, as opposed to the harmful outlets that they are all too often already acquainted with.

This process will often include a full discussion of the unique things that trigger each person's anger. The overarching purpose of this process is to educate everyone to be more aware of their emotions at all times and at every degree of anger intensity. Consequently, this process will frequently include a detailed discussion of the things that trigger each person's anger. The end objective is for them to learn how to utilize these indications as a guide to assist them in maintaining better control of their anger.

This kind of supervised therapeutic setting is not only for those people who are dealing with anger problems directly; it is also for those people who are coping with the aftermath of having spent too much time with individuals whose anger issues remain unresolved. The reason for this is that anger is contagious; if one person vents their rage on another, the target of that fury is more than likely to lash back in like. And as a result, this contributes to an increase in rage around the globe.

Anger management treatment is not intended to "cure" anger, but rather to equip individuals who are struggling with anger issues with as many alternative choices as possible for coping with their problems. The purpose of anger management therapy is not to "cure" anger. The goal of anger management treatment is to teach patients new ways to deal with distressing feelings. This is due to the fact that behaving aggressively in response to anything makes whatever justification you may have had for being furious in the first place invalid. Additionally, it may make it simpler to look at circumstances from alternative aspects that are progressively more effective.

There are one-on-one and group settings for anger management therapy, while the one-on-one sessions generally include a group component as well.

Anger management treatment may be found in both of these settings. It is probable that certain aspects of the patient's anger problems may be addressed during individual sessions. These aspects may include things like rage connected to job, troubles with relationships, or concerns with families. If you are unable to successfully get your issues under control on your own and you allow your anger issues to grow out of control, then you may find yourself in a situation where the court orders you to attend one of these types of classes as a result of domestic violence or other legal issues. If you are unable to successfully get your issues under control on your own, then you may allow your anger issues to grow out of control.

Classes on anger management, in contrast to certain forms of treatment, do not mandate a certain number of sessions or hours of attendance. Instead, the patient and the therapist will be the ones to decide what problems need to be addressed and when the lessons will no longer be necessary in the end. It is typical practice in many anger management programs to give participants homework assignments or other chores to do while they are actively participating in the program. These are meant to reinforce the strategies and principles that were covered in the primary session and ensure that the participant does not fall behind in their understanding throughout the course of the week. However, perhaps the most essential aspect of these activities is that they provide the participant with opportunities to apply what they have learned in authentic settings.

Both in-person and online classes on anger management are made available by the National Anger Management Association (NAM) across the continental United States. It is the main organization in the field of dealing with anger problems, and it certifies everyone from psychiatrists to religious leaders to life coaches who are interested in efficiently looking out and dealing with the many sorts of anger issues that exist.

Sadly, even though anger management treatment is effective for a large number of individuals, it is not a silver bullet that can solve these problems overnight. This is particularly true if the problems are the result of learned habits that have been present since childhood. To get the most out of these kinds of seminars, you have to be prepared to put in the effort on your end and have a genuine desire to make changes in your life. If you don't have the drive to become better, you'll just wind up staying in the same spot.

Our Tempers Are Quick To Flare By Nature.

Then there are certain individuals who just have short fused temperaments. You are aware of who I am referring to. It's possible that you are one of them, or that you just know other individuals who fit that description. But regardless of that, the conduct is probably something you've seen before. A person with a very short temper is characterized by a number of behaviors, including but not limited to, losing control of their temper with little to no provocation, shouting at others for no apparent reason, and losing their patience at the drop of a hat.

It doesn't take much to get this kind of person upset; just about anything may set them off, which is why other people have a tendency to see them as challenging individuals to deal with. If you know someone like this, you are aware that you have to walk on eggshells around them for fear of getting on their (very!) bad side. If you know someone like this, you also know that you need to tiptoe around them. Obviously, you shouldn't spend your life like that, but what other options do you have? No one enjoys being yelled at, particularly when there is no need for the person to be yelled at in the first place.

This has the potential to generate a great deal of contention in a variety of settings, including those involving the family as well as the workplace. Who hasn't heard the nightmare tales of the unreasonable and crazy boss? It's possible that you, too, are having trouble with this. Because it's not something you can control, dealing with it may be quite challenging at times. If controlling your anger is something you are struggling with, all you have to do is keep reading, and not only will you be able to discover some answers, but you will also be able to get some assistance. This is exactly why I chose to produce this e-book on anger management.

As you can see, the issue is not so much with a particular person or a certain component as it is with the circumstance itself the most of the time. It is obvious that stressful events cannot be avoided all of the time; but, if you are aware that you are more likely to get angry when you are really exhausted, for example, you may take efforts to prevent an episode of rage and the potential problems that might result from it.

Stay away from people and any known triggers.

Do not do jobs that need a high degree of accuracy or that are sensitive in any other way if you are in a high-pressure scenario.

Avoid participating in any diplomatic discussions.

Do not engage in conversation with those with whom you disagree. If you are provoked, ignore it or leave the room.

You should avoid looking for trouble.

Avoid escalating a quarrel that is already ongoing.

Do not engage in activities that need a lot of patience or your whole focus.

You should put off really critical duties, projects, or assignments until you are well-rested and have a clear brain.

Do not make decisions under the influence of emotion.

Learn to reign in your compulsions.

Take a step back and examine the situation with an impartial eye.

Take a rest, and maybe even a nap, if you need to.

Don't be stubborn about something if it's not working out the way you hoped it would; come back to it later.

Issues Of A Physcial Nature That Result From Being Angry

Cortisol is a hormone that is secreted by the body in response to negative emotions such as anger. Your body's chemistry may be significantly altered as a result of this. Anger may not only bring about health difficulties for the one who is acting aggressively, but it can also cause damage to other individuals.

In the course of their research, the authors of one study sought to answer the question, "How does being physically abused as a child affect one's mental and physical health in midlife?" Additionally, the moderating influence of family history and early challenges was investigated in this study.

The outcomes were disastrous to say the least. The findings of the study showed a correlation between childhood physical abuse and increased levels of depressive symptoms, anxiety, and rage. In addition to this, it predicted poor health, as well as a wide variety of particular medical diagnoses and physical symptoms (Springer et al., 2007).

You need to be able to determine for yourself whether or not you are going to let the fact that someone is upset with you affect you. You have the option of allowing it to make you angry and frantic to find a solution to the problem. You might also come to the conclusion that you should not let their wrath disturb you since it is their problem to solve, not yours. However, children lack the emotional intelligence necessary to identify the appropriate frame of mind for the second scenario. They often behave in a manner that imitates the feelings of those in authority over them or reacts in a secondary manner to those feelings. When kids observe adults in distress, it will cause them to feel the same way.

Consider the scenario in which a youngster stumbles and falls, and the parent tries to maintain their composure despite the fact that their child has suffered an injury. Even if the circumstance may be somewhat alarming depending on the nature of the injury, the kid may start to sob even more and get more unhappy if the parent begins to freak out and become distressed. Even though adults have a difficult time understanding their feelings, children have an even more difficult time doing so.

In addition, anger may be a contributor to ongoing pain. After all, being furious causes you to often keep your muscles in a tense state, clench your jaw, clasp your fists tightly, and strain your shoulders. If you never give your body a chance to really unwind and rest, it will eventually start to give you a lot of trouble.

Irritable bowel syndrome (IBS), another frequent health concern that persons who suffer chronic rage often have, will be discussed further down in this article (Pilowsky, 1976).

IBS

When you are under persistent stress, the hormone cortisol will be released, which will cause an increase in the amount of acid that is produced in your stomach. In addition to having an effect on your esophagus and intestines, it also has the potential to give you an ulcer.

One research compared patients with BS to people with an organic bowel ailment (Crohn's disease) in order to discover whether or not patients with BS exhibit greater levels of trait and repressed anger. In addition to this, the researchers wanted to determine whether or not these factors act as a mediator in the connection between abuse and IBS (Beesley et al., 2010). The findings showed that individuals with IBS had higher levels of both trait and repressed anger than those with BS. After adjusting for a variety of other psychological factors as well, the differences in trait anger remained statistically significant. In addition, patients with IBS had a higher prevalence of childhood sexual abuse than patients with Crohn's disease, although this did not have any connection to trait anger.

Because of this, harboring resentment may cause quite a significant degree of discomfort in the stomach.

When It Comes Down To It, There Is Just One Approach That Will Work For Anger Management.

There will always be those individuals who seem to be more furious than others, or who are more prone to anger in comparison to others, regardless of whether or not anger is regarded to be a natural emotion in humans. In addition to this, they lack the capacity to regulate their emotions, which might lead to unfavorable consequences. The term "anger management" will be defined, and some of the fundamentals associated with it will be discussed in this chapter.

Why is it that certain people's tempers are so easily roused?

Even while anger is a normal emotion that everyone experiences at some point, there are certain individuals who are more prone to experiencing it than others.

These individuals, according to the opinions of the experts, have a poor frustration tolerance. As a result, circumstances that elicit a moderate level of annoyance in the vast majority of people might be very unpleasant for some individuals and potentially elicit a strong response from them.

An further rationale for this conduct may be found in the individual's family history, and more specifically in their interactions to their family members. If the individual originates from a dysfunctional family or if the members of the family are unable to transmit their feelings in an appropriate way, it is quite probable that the individual will struggle with both managing and expressing their emotions.

There are some individuals who were born and seen to readily become irritated during their childhood years; this may be a sign that the same would be witnessed from them as they get older. Genes can also play a factor, as there are others who were born and observed to easily get upset throughout their adult years.

Because the majority of people have been socialized to believe that unpleasant emotions should not be expressed openly, most individuals have developed a tendency to repress them. However, at some point in the future, it will become intolerable for the person, which may lead to even more negative repercussions.

How To Handle Angry Feelings

According to the teachings of the Bible, we need to get rid of wrath, hatred, malice, slander, and language that is vulgar. God does not instruct us to discover methods to control our terrible anger, to indulge it or to get used to it in any manner. God will not ask us to do anything that is impossible for us to do. And more significantly, it is to our benefit that we deal with these loopholes since they are capable of preventing us from completing the plans that God has for our life. This is why dealing with these loopholes is to our advantage.

If you really want to, you can get over your anger problems right now. Stop making excuses for yourself and accept responsibility for your actions, then pray to God for assistance. You can learn to control your wrath, yes. If you ask God for the ability to perform what you need to, He will certainly provide it. As you continue to obey, the power of God will be made available to you for the completion of the victory that was won for you at the cross.

If you feel ready to confront your anger, the following are some strategies that might help you get started...

1. Reflect on the role that anger plays in your life.

We have established throughout this book that anger is a significant problem. It has the potential to take a person's life as well as the lives of those around them. It's not a little matter that we can easily solve by just exercising more self-control and acquiring some new psychological strategies. It's a dangerous tool in the devil's arsenal, with the end goal of robbing, killing, and destroying people here on earth, and ultimately preventing people from joining the kingdom of God.

Learn to see anger in the same way that the Bible does. Do not make light of the situation. Recognize that anger is a formidable foe that requires careful management on your part in order to prevent it from causing harm to you and others around you.

2. Recognize the rage that is inside you.

The Bible warns that those who try to hide their shortcomings will not be successful. However, if we acknowledge our wrongdoing and turn away from it, we will receive compassion and find healing (Proverbs 28:13; 1 John 1:9).

Don't make an effort to ignore or calm your rage. Be honest with yourself, and with God, by telling yourself the truth. If we do not confess our wrongdoing, we will not be able to get assistance.

Putting Your Mindfulness Into Practice

Today, all you need to do is allow yourself some time to meditate and focus on the here and now. Perform some exercises that focus on your breath. Find an area in your house that is calm and peaceful, set a mat there, and sit down. Focus on nothing except your breathing while you do this. You can nurture a healthy mind via mindfulness, and having a healthy, quiet mind may help you feel at ease even in challenging circumstances, which in turn makes it easier for you to maintain control over your emotions. Yoga and other forms of slow, gentle exercise may be beneficial. The muscles in your body may become more relaxed via the practice of yoga, which in turn can help you feel more at ease.

The practice of being mindful is essentially a sort of meditation. When you meditate, you should concentrate on the feeling of your breathing as it travels to different parts of your body. You are able to take note of your ideas as they come to mind when you are able to concentrate on your breath. You are then able to let go of thoughts that you are always dealing with in the back of your mind when you are able to let go of those thoughts. This makes you more aware of the fact that such ideas often arise, as well as the fact that such thoughts do not constitute who you are. You may imagine your ideas coming into being like a bubble, and then exploding as they are extinguished. Feelings and ideas, whether positive and negative, are only fleeting. They occur, and it is up to you to decide whether or not you will act on them.

It is observation without judgment or commentary. You need to have compassion for yourself and refrain from being too harsh on yourself. Instead of taking things so personally and letting it get to you, you will learn how to see negative emotions, such as worry or dissatisfaction, as passing storm clouds and observe as they pass away. You may basically learn how to take control of your negative thinking pattern so that it doesn't wind up throwing you into a downward spiral as a result of it. It enables you to have complete dominion over your own thoughts and feelings.

To get things rolling, Put your hands down on your thighs in a relaxed manner. Your eyes should be slightly open, and you should focus your gaze on a spot on the ground in front of you. You should direct your focus onto the wall in front of you if you have one. Maintain a calm and collected look. It's not directed at one particular thing; rather, it's more like looking into the void. It shouldn't do anything except relax.

Begin by doing nothing more than just sitting there in the setting you've constructed. If you notice that your mind is starting to wander, draw it back to the present moment as gently as possible. It is normal for your mind to wander, which is why you need to bring it back to the here and now in a calm and deliberate manner.

The second component of practicing mindfulness is paying attention to your breath. When you begin your next session of meditation, after you have found a comfortable position and have settled in, give just a passing attention to your breathing. Take note of how it affects you both as you draw in and as you let out your breath. There is no extra action required of you in any way. You are just concentrating on how you now are, rather than how you can alter the way that you are breathing. If you become aware that you are attempting to regulate your breathing, release your grip on it. When you first begin, it will be difficult, so try not to concentrate on whether or not your breath is natural.

Putting your attention on your thoughts is the third component of the mindfulness practice. You will discover that when you are sitting still and meditating, many ideas will enter your mind. There may be occasions when a few of your ideas will run into each other and overlap one another. This may be a plan, a memory, a song from a television ad, or a fantasy. Because of your thoughts, you can have the impression that you can't even concentrate on taking a deep breath. This happens rather often, particularly with those who are just starting off with their meditation practice. Taking note of how you are feeling is the most crucial thing.

Rule No. 4: Maintain an open line of communication

There is no strategy that is more effective than maintaining open lines of communication, regardless of how frustrated you are with the other person.

If your next-door neighbors are constantly disturbing your peaceful slumbers at home by being noisy and unpleasant, rather than becoming upset and judgemental with them, you could attempt talking to them in order to get them to respect your personal space and limits. Take a rational approach to dealing with them, such as saying, "Hey, I'm aware that you have a big family, and I know that there is bound to be some commotion because you have kids." I fully get that; but, I would ask that you keep in mind that I put in a lot of effort during the day, and that I am in desperate need of my sleep. If it's at all possible, I'd really appreciate it if you could attempt to keep a lower profile in the nights.

There is a good chance that your neighbor was unaware that their behavior was bothering you, but they will make an effort to be quieter when they see you at home.

Communication is the most valuable asset that humans possess, and maintaining an open mind may facilitate the development of new possibilities that would not have been possible had the person been angry.

Rule number five: Let it out

When I say "let out your anger," what I mean is "let it out through a healthier outlet than getting angry and taking revenge," since that is not what I mean by "let out your anger." A lot of people already know that doing some exercise is a good way to channel negative emotions like anger and frustration. Therefore, the next time you feel yourself furious or on the verge of fury, immediately pack your gear and go to the gym that is most convenient for you. Alternately, you could just go for a run, a jog, or engage in some light, free-hand exercise right where you are. This would be a good option.

It's probable that this won't always be achievable, particularly if you're already at work, it's already late, or the timing isn't right. even you feel that you are becoming irritated in these kinds of circumstances, you should make an effort to remove yourself from the issue, even only for the time being. Take a break for a half an hour and go get a cup of coffee by yourself, go into the other room and put on some relaxing music, or do anything you want—cook, clean, whatever.

If you are creative, put your anger into your work instead of venting it on other people. You could find that drawing, singing, or playing some music helps you to relax. Some individuals find it helpful to write down what's upsetting them on paper, while others try their hand at writing poetry about how they're feeling.

How To Control Your Angry Emotions

You are going to want to do all in your power to steer clear of a circumstance that will put your patience to the test. It's possible that you won't always be able to pull this off, but you'd be astonished at how much strife and anger you can sidestep if you simply give it a go. Even while you can't always control what other people say around you, there are things you can do to make it less likely that you'll lose your cool.

What gets your blood boiling?

Everyone has their own unique take on how the line "I always hate it when..." is supposed to be finished. There are certain triggers that make sense, while others do not. The important thing to remember, though, is that they are more likely to irritate you than anything else.

Do you consider yourself to be the kind of person that despises really loud noises? Do you not appreciate it when other people handle your belongings? Do you find it annoying when others at work refer to you by an inappropriate nickname? Not only on the level of habits, but also on the level of self-awareness, it is extremely necessary that you be familiar with these things. This indicates that you are aware of the specifics of this "peeve" of yours as well as the reasons why it drives you crazy. You might question some of your closest friends about it, or you could just attempt to go back to occasions when you became upset and find out what triggered that outburst in the first place.

It's important to keep in mind that anger may be sparked by a variety of factors all at once, but in most cases, it's sparked by a single factor and then just increases from there. When it comes to taking preventative measures, it is helpful to have an understanding of what first irritated the other person.

When you have it mastered, the following are some things that you may do to rectify that situation:

First, you should try to reason out whether or not the things that irritate you should. You'd be astonished to learn how many little and pointless things may drive us to anger. In all honesty, the most effective method for overcoming them is to just acquire the ability to brush them aside.

Do you really need to let it affect you that much? In any case, how much harm does it cause? A lot of those little things are just things that we have developed a pattern of reacting negatively to out of habit.

It's possible that the folks that aggravate you aren't even aware that they're doing so. It's possible that they're simply joking around, or maybe that's just how they are in general. You have to be the better person sometimes and simply learn to accept certain individuals whose behavior is less pleasant than others'.

Second, is there a straightforward solution to the problem? Is it possible that something you haven't tried yet may have been the solution to the issue all along?

You should always give folks who have a pattern of irritating you the benefit of the doubt and attempt to have a conversation with them. Tell them that you find it annoying when they bring up a topic that causes you to feel uneasy and that you don't want it discussed. Inform them that there are some items in your room, on your desk, or in some other personal location that they are not allowed to touch in any way.

If the other side does not comply, you always have the option of bringing the issue up with someone else who you believe can assist you (for example, a mutual friend who is respected by both parties, your supervisor or another person in a position of power, etc.).

Dealing with the other little issues that you have, such as the clutter on your desk or the squeaky sound that your chair creates, is something that you should simply go ahead and do. There are instances when we choose to ignore the annoyances that are occurring around us, which ultimately leads to the escalation of problematic circumstances. The remainder of your day will be easier to bear if you give yourself permission to get away from the stressful situation for a while in order to address the issues that need to be addressed. Always keep in mind what may work out better for you in the long term.

Find strategies to steer clear of problems that you are unable to solve, improve, or otherwise make better. It's possible that you may rearrange your work schedule in such a manner as to avoid coming into contact with the coworker who irritates you the most when you're in the office. whether the environment where you usually work or study is constantly too loud, you should see whether there are other, more peaceful options available to you.

The lesson to be learned from all of this is straightforward: don't disregard the things that get under your skin and make you angry. Instead, you should identify the problems and attempt to solve them if you can; if this is not possible, you should steer clear of the remaining problems. The next chapters will assist you in dealing with anything else related to this topic.

Prepare Yourself!

You know from your own experience that there are certain times of the day or other specific circumstances that will put your patience to the test. These situations may be anything from traffic to a change in the weather. You may be aware that the workplace is about to enter its busiest time of year, which means that everyone's nerves are going to be on edge. Or maybe you're ready to go to a social event that you never intended to go to in the first place because you don't get along with the other people who are coming. It is important to keep in mind that you have more influence on the events occurring around you than you may realize, and you should make the most of this fact.

You should, for one thing, see these events as significant causes of stress, which, in turn, might make your composure more difficult to maintain. Therefore, it is essential that you tackle these challenges in the best physical state possible. This implies heading in that direction without letting any other concerns distract you at the present. This also involves going into the situation having eaten recently, having had sufficient rest, and maybe even having showered.

If you are not prepared, you can always find methods to postpone your exposure until you feel like you are in the mood to take on additional stress. If you are not prepared, you can always find ways to delay your exposure. If it's an appointment for work, make sure you get some rest before going, especially if you just came back from an equally stressful situation. If your secretary or a coworker comes up to you and informs you about an issue, you should ask if it is possible for it to wait and then explain that you will assist them in solving the situation after a little while.

What more can you do than take some deep breaths, relax with a cup of coffee (or anything else that helps you unwind), and take some time out for yourself to enjoy some downtime? You have the ability to get yourself psychologically ready for the circumstance. It will be much simpler for you to handle what you are about to deal with if you are fully aware that it contains a lot of unexpected and unpleasant happenings. This will make it much easier for you to cope with what you are about to deal with than it would be if you went into the scene having no information whatsoever. Imagine that you are getting ready to take a punch—somehow, your body is making itself ready to take that blow. This is analogous to what is happening.

And the answer is yes, you will at some point have to take that blow, regardless of how well prepared you are. present that you're here, it's time to figure out what to do while you're really in the present.

Keep A Record Of Your Wrath In A Diary.

It is possible that people may be able to better forecast triggers and regulate their reactions if they keep a journal of their furious feelings and describe what happened before, during, and after an event.

By gaining an understanding of which methods of self-control were successful and which were not, it may be possible to build a method of anger management that is more efficient.

Don't stifle the feelings that are driving your wrath; doing so will just make it worse. Instead, after you've gained control of your emotions, communicate how you are feeling in a way that is self-assured and non-aggressive. Keeping a journal might be an effective method for accomplishing this goal.

A person who writes may also find it easier to recognize and adjust thoughts that contribute to inappropriate levels of rage.

Altering your thought processes from those that are final or catastrophic to those that are more practical and constructive may be good.

Altering the statement "Everything is wrecked" to read "This is frustrating, but a resolution is available" may help clarify the problem and increase the possibility that a solution may be found.

The symptoms

As a person's level of anger rises from mild irritation to full-blown rage, they are more likely to experience the following:

- An intense need to remove oneself from the problematic situation

- Sensitivity issues

- Melancholy or depressive feelings on your part

- Remorse

- The emotion of resentment

- A feeling of unease

- The impulse to lash out in some fashion, either verbally or physically

There is a possibility that you may also experience any of the following physical symptoms:

- Rubbing the palm of one's hand across one's face and/or cheeks

- Acting restless and clasping one hand in the other, for example, as a kind of fidgeting.

- Going in circles back and forth

- Criticism, sarcasm, impoliteness, or abrasive language

- They no longer have a good sense of humor.

- A need for drugs, such as alcohol, cigarettes, or narcotics, that the person feels would provide them the serenity they want but which they are unable to get.

- Raising either your volume or your pitch when you speak

· Crying out loud or wailing

Additionally, a person could exhibit the following symptoms:

- An discomfort in the stomach

- A quicker rate of heartbeat

- Being very sweaty

- Breathing that is shallow and rapid

- Spikes in temperature in the head, face, or neck

- Trembling in the hands, lips, or jaws

- a sensation of spinning

- A prickling or tingling feeling at the nape of your neck

It is possible for a person to use their management abilities in order to keep the situation under control if they are able to recognize intense anger or pain in the current moment.

Dangerous Obstacles

It would seem that human curiosity has replaced all other potentially dangerous tendencies. We show our displeasure at them for a handful of transgressions and pay them interest on an ongoing basis while also imposing restrictions on the best way to navigate the situation. In addition, we are concerned that our children may be permanently traumatized if the watchmen engage in combat before them. Anyway, what could possibly be completed? Does it make sense for us to speak about it, ponder about it, or even picture it if it now no longer exists? Does it even make sense to do any of those things? None of these choices are very sound ones. The problem is not that amazement exists; the problem is with the way that we talk about it. There is no room for doubt about the fact that continuous, rapid shifts, disputes, and shifts in mood are terrible for our economic growth. It puts us into the "fight or flight" mode, which means that adrenaline is flowing through our bodies and that we are on high alert for any potential danger. When this happens, the body goes into a fully prepared state, which increases the risk of high blood pressure, blocked conductors, and therefore the possibility of a stroke and respiratory depression. it is very clear that, in the aftermath of having our frustrations vented, we need to giving vent to our anger.

We are saddened by a number of or all of the following topics:

• A sizeable percentage of individuals have been conditioned to reveal their innermost thoughts and feelings to at least one representative of the following:

• Trying to convey awe and amazement to people is both difficult and painful.

- *Even if we are upset and trying to get out of it, it is banned.*

- *Even if we are upset and believe that it will result in an exception, we are prohibited from doing so.*

- *We do not have the ability to lose our ability to control other people.*

- *Inadequacy is the opposite of outrage.*

- *Shouting at top volume and acting cruelly are the two most effective ways to instill awe in someone.*

- *It is possible that an awful person might be any character in the story who is angry.*

- *Married couples should never, under any circumstances, get some near eye angry.*

- *A normal parent will never lose their cool with their kid and yell at them.*

- *Happily married folks do not at all tend to put on weight.*

- *Being sensitive to another person's discomfort is a sign of unity.*

It's possible that you believe the active symptoms of stun-related difficulties are limited to wonder, but certain anxious states should show you that you're really failing to manage wonder in a safe and sound manner. There is a possibility that your energy may display persistent irritability, wrath, and tension. If you often feel overwhelmed, have difficulties keeping your thoughts organized or locating them, or daydream about killing yourself or other people, you may be suffering from a depression disorder or another mental health issue.

Intelligence pertaining to the emotions

Being aware of one's own feelings is what is meant by the term "emotional awareness." You need to be aware of the things that are going on around you, but more importantly, you need to be conscious of the thoughts that are going through your head and the emotions that you are experiencing. It is only by doing so that you will be able to effectively handle them.

The expression of your intelligence is not restricted to how well you do in your professional or academic life. Emotional intelligence is just as vital as logical intelligence. It has garnered popularity all around the globe, and in the same way that the intelligence quotient (IQ) assesses intellect, the emotional intelligence quotient (EQ) measures emotional intelligence. You need to work on improving your emotional intelligence in addition to learning anger management skills if you want to be successful.

The capacity to regulate, observe, and assess one's own emotions is what we mean when we talk about emotional intelligence. We've been hearing for years that it's important to try to understand things from other people's points of view and to develop empathy for those around us. If you aren't conscious of the things that cause you stress and the methods in which you control yourself, this may be a challenging task. Your ability to control your anger, sympathize with others, develop deeper relationships, and achieve your objectives are all things that may be helped by improving your emotional intelligence.

Increasing your self-awareness and emotional intelligence may be accomplished in a number of ways, including the following:

Regain command of your own state of being.

People who are emotionally intelligent almost always exhibit this quality to a significant degree. They are conscious of themselves. You will develop a greater awareness of your emotions as you develop a greater awareness of yourself. Pay attention to your body language and how you respond to different circumstances so that you may determine for yourself what causes you the greatest stress.

Put a name to how you're feeling.

You have to give credence to whatever it is that you are experiencing now at this exact second. Just focus on the here and now, and don't worry about the past or the future; just be mindful of who you are right now. Are you under a lot of stress? Do you suffer from anxiety? You have to admit that you feel whatever it is that you feel. You have to direct your attention within and pay attention to what is going on there.

It is possible for anger to cover over other feelings, such as humiliation or shame, at times. You should be putting all of your attention on yourself. Label your feelings, but don't assign positive or negative connotations to them. Simply bring your attention to the emotions you're experiencing now at this precise second. Because of this, it could be simpler for you to recognize your sentiments in a hurry.

Dealing With The Physical Effects Of Angry, Stressful, And Anxious Thoughts And Feelings

When these three "monsters" are staring at you, it is possible that you may experience physical discomfort as well as changes in your body's physiological state. You've already discovered, via reading the first few chapters of this book, that the brain is the primary factor in determining how your feelings are expressed. It is due to the fact that your brain is able to activate the hormones and chemical substances that create pain as well as changes in the body's physiology.

You have also learned how to modify the way that you think, which means that you are now able to change the way that you feel in order to better control your anger, worry, and stress. This indicates that if you are successful in altering the way that you think, you won't have any issues controlling these three essential facets of your life.

You should be prepared for the fact that, during the first few days of putting the ideas from this book into practice, you will not always be successful. Because of this, you will need to be familiar with how to deal with clinical symptoms in the event that they manifest themselves. Hopefully, this will not happen very often. Let's talk about the most prominent symptoms. These are the actions that you need to do. These only apply to you if you don't have any significant underlying diseases, such as heart problems, AIDS, or organ impairments. In the event that your symptoms are really severe, you should seek medical attention.

Symptoms may include fast or labored breathing, often known as hyperventilation or dyspnea.

Rapid breathing may lead to a condition known as respiratory alkalosis, which is an acid-base imbalance. Because of this disease, the blood's pH level (which measures acidity and alkalinity) rises, becoming more alkaline. The condition known as alkalosis is brought on by the excessive exhalation of the acidic component carbon dioxide by the body. If treatment is not received, this may lead to coma and ultimately death.

What must be done

Get a paper bag out of your bag and put it over your lips. Take a few deep breaths in and out of the paper bag. This will enable the carbon dioxide that you exhaled to be reabsorbed by your body when you subsequently inhale it again. The situation in which this is most helpful is when the individual is hyperventilating as a result of his feelings.

After you have slept for a few hours in bed and worked through the breathing exercises, your breathing should return to normal.

Abuse of force

What must be done

Exercise self-control and get out of there as soon as possible. Consider the constructive actions that you have been mentally portraying to yourself on a consistent basis. You are free to go to the restroom or any other room that is suitable and practice your breathing exercises there. In the event that you are unable to carry it out openly, do it covertly wherever you are. In the event that there is a cut or a bruise, you should respond to it as soon as possible by cleaning the affected region of the body and applying pressure. If it has to be stitched, you should go to the clinic that is located closest to you in the surrounding region.

Do You Think You Owe It? Here Are Some Tips To Help You Get Over The Guilt You Feel After Losing Your Cool With Your Children.

It's not the end of the world if you lose your cool with your child once in a while. You shouldn't let that one thing define who you are. In addition, this in no way indicates that you are a poor parent in any manner. Take a few slow, deep breaths and calm down the next time you find yourself feeling bad about losing your temper with your child.

I get it; despite your best efforts to never lose your composure and have a level head at all times, you still found yourself losing your cool. I want you to know that what you're experiencing is typical. And despite the fact that you are making every attempt to prevent it, it will nonetheless occur on occasion.

If, despite your best attempts to prevent emotional outbursts against your children, you find that you have lost it, here are five things you can do to help you get over the guilty feeling and go on with your life.

Here is a list of five things to do after yelling at your children.

1. Take A Deep Breath: When you were in an angry mood, your body was tight, your pulse was rapid, your breathing was snappy, and your brain was confused. When you take a deep breath, you may calm your body and clear your mind. Just take a few slow, deep breaths to see if it helps calm your racing thoughts and restore some equilibrium to your body, mind, and spirit.

Do not utter another word or take another action until you have taken a few full breaths. It will assist in settling your nerves and will make you feel somewhat better overall.

2.) Be on the lookout for the re-trigger: children will always behave like children. And that means they will push you to your limit a couple of more times than they already have. Have you ever shouted at someone to stop doing something annoying, and then a few of minutes later, they continued doing what they were doing? That's what you get when you have kids!

Always be on the lookout for such a predicament, and constantly remind yourself that you are in control of both your actions and your feelings. Forget the fact that you lost it a few minutes ago or not quite long ago (whatever time it was), and persuade yourself that this time you won't let it slip through your fingers. Repeat to yourself again and over and over again how true that statement is. Also, maintain your composure and keep cool.

3. Acknowledge That You Are Completely Responsible For Your Angry Reaction: It doesn't matter whose fault it is; whether your children disobeyed your instructions or not, acknowledge that you are completely responsible for whatever occurred.

In addition to the punishment they need, you need to show your children how to accept responsibility for their actions without shifting the blame. You may do this by apologizing to them and stating something along the lines of "Oops, I'm so sorry about losing that. It wasn't right of me."

Don't attempt to bring it up again after you've once apologized to them. Let go and go on with your life.

4.) Act Promptly to Repair Your Relationship With Them If you have ever spoken harsh words to your children or imposed severe penalties on them, it is natural for them to pull away from you and separate themselves from you. However, if you act quickly, you can repair your relationship with them.

When something like this occurs, you should shelve the problem for the time being and concentrate on repairing your connection with the person in question.

Always keep in mind that the goal is not to make them feel less of themselves or to damage the connection with them, but rather to assist them in developing into better humans. And this is something you are able to do when you have a healthy connection with them.

5.) Look for Patterns: once your outburst, instead of putting it off and pretending it never occurred, give yourself some time to go about the scenario once again once you've calmed down. This will help you look for patterns, which may help you avoid having future outbursts.

Find out what caused you to react the way you did. Was it a specific word or phrase that your child uttered? What kind of feelings did it give you? Look through all of them to see if you can see a pattern that causes you to behave in such a manner and see if you can identify it.

Home-Based Work Involving The Use Of Triggers

When you're dealing with rage triggers at home, it might seem like you're climbing the biggest mountain of them all at times. Because they set them up, members of your family are familiar with how to use your buttons, as was just described. Your home is, in a way, a major source of potential annoyance just waiting to be triggered. This is not simply another instance of the "you always hurt the one you love" mentality. It is about how severe the rivalry that is indicated inside a home or extended family is for affection, connection, resources, food, clothes, care, and everything else that we need. In a home when things are generally going well, we are able to meet all of the fundamental requirements that are required to maintain at least some level of composure among the members of the household. On the other hand, even in a family where everyone seems to be doing well, there is still a good chance that at least one member of the household may have the impression that their requirements are not being satisfied. At that moment, the anger reaction becomes vital in having that need satisfied, and since it may easily go astray, it has to be controlled. since of the ease with which it can go awry, it needs to be handled.

What kinds of triggers do individuals experience while they are in their own homes? To put it simply, there are an infinite number of them. It's possible that the youngster is still wide awake despite the parent's insistence that it's time for bed. It's possible that one parent doesn't want to cook while the other parent does all the cooking, which leads to animosity between the two of them over time. It is possible that siblings are fighting with one other, which triggers the anger reaction, while the parents have two different views of how to discipline their children, which results in everyone being in a state of disarray. It's possible that one adult sibling may be envious of the other and behave out in hostile or passive-aggressive ways, which would result in a breakdown in communication between the two of them. It's possible that a parent has reservations about the person their kid is dating. The person whom a kid's single parent is dating is not someone the youngster endorses. Whether they are simply perceived wants or genuine needs, the limbic brain and the reptile brain are always on the lookout for needs that are not being satisfied. This is true whether the needs are perceived or actual.

This is where the proverbial "rubber meets the road" when it comes to the many different life domains. A person's perceived or actual unmet needs are the single most important factor in determining whether or not they will experience rage. This factor is even more important than loss and despair. We are always on the lookout for ways to ensure our survival, whether it be for financial goods or for a desired value such as respect, whether it be a need for a new automobile or for justice to finally be served in the world; whatever it may be, we are always on the search. Anger that is not well handled may, over time, lead to an expansion of the group of people, locations, objects, and ideas that are seen as essential for continued life. This is not to suggest that not all of the things that make us furious are, in reality, about our ability to stay alive. People who are upset about social justice, people who are angry because they lost their house or their income, people who are outraged about any number of true life-or-death situations – this is our anger addressing real unmet needs, and it can provide the fuel to have our needs addressed if it is utilized correctly. On the other hand, when the sense of life-or-death necessities begins to seep into other domains, this is often the moment when rage takes control of the situation, creates the plans, and leads the procession. When we start down this path, we may not even be aware of or understand why we are beginning to mistakenly bypass our cognitive skills in the decision-making process. This may be a vicious cycle.

When one is at home, everything seems to be about surviving. It is the location in which we have all come to the conclusion that the primary objective of our group should be to survive. We may learn the art of living rather than just surviving if we include effective tactics for the control of our anger into the equation.

If this system is going to be able to get back on its feet, each person who is a part of it has to take responsibility for managing the part of the system that pertains to them. In the event that you are the one who is angry, you need to deal with the feelings that your rage is hiding, such as fear, anxiousness, sadness, guilt, shame, aloneness, emptiness, forlornness, shock, despair, or vulnerability over other people and situations.

Using your anger to try to gain control over other people is almost always a projection of your own internal identity's frustration with you for not dealing with yourself in some way, and this frustration is directed at you. How is it that you are avoiding taking responsibility for yourself? What aspects of your life do you delegate to other people, and then become angry over when they don't carry out their responsibilities properly?

As long as you allow yourself to believe that taking out your frustrations on other people is acceptable behavior, you will continue to do it. When you finally come to the realization that the psychological darts of rage are almost as dangerous to another person as actual physical darts, you will finally put an end to your behavior. As long as you continue to give your wounded self permission to take charge whenever your agonizing feelings surface, you will not be able to let go of your anger. When you have practiced Inner Bonding for a long enough period of time to have an adoring grown-up present whenever the anguish arises, you will, fortunately, be in a position to choose how you react to it.

If you are the pleasant, safe, or withdrawn one, you need to recognize that you are not taking loving thought of yourself either, even if you are the one who is the most agreeable, secure, or withdrawn. Instead of being responsive by caving in, resisting, withdrawing, or becoming upset as a consequence of these behaviors, you should confront the fact that it is unacceptable for other people to unload their wrath onto you. You need to speak out and let the angry person know that you are not available to discuss any problem while they are using anger as a way for coping with conflict. You need to make it clear that you are unavailable to do so.

Keeping Control Of Our Angry Moods And Our Children

There are, of course, a variety of different scenarios in which a parent could get frustrated with their offspring. The strain we experience at work may very easily seep into our personal life. Conflicts between parents are another potential contributing factor. It's possible that the pressure of their finances is getting to them. Simply the pressure of having to be a good parent is enough to send a person completely insane. Any one of these possibilities may be what set off your current state of annoyance. When your irritation escalates into anger, you should consider looking for any way to calm down. The following are some strategies that might help you control your anger toward your children:

When you find yourself becoming angry, try to remain calm first.

When you sense anger building up inside of you, resist the need to respond immediately away. Instantly reacting to the circumstance won't do anything except make things more difficult for you and your children. Do not react as if the situation you are dealing with is an emergency since it is very likely that it is not. Instead, give yourself a moment to just breathe. In order for you to think clearly, your brain requires oxygen. After you've had a chance to catch your breath and assess the situation, it's time to choose how you want to proceed. If you are composed yourself, it will be much simpler for you to instill composure in your kid and impart wisdom to them.

Asking yourself, "What Am I Angry About?" is a good place to start.

There is a good chance that the anger you feel towards your kid is not, in fact, anger at all. Anger is most likely being used as an outlet for other feelings, such as grief, disappointment, fear, and maybe even other feelings. When you have a clear understanding of the nature of the issue at hand, you will be more equipped to find a solution.

Establish Personal Boundaries Regarding How Much You Can Put Up With.

It is better to take care of this business before you become furious, rather than when you are fuming within. How much of a certain conduct are you ready to put up with before you draw the line? Do not allow the situation to spiral out of control. Instead, try redirecting your children's attention to something that will cause you less frustration. For instance, maybe your children like playing together, but there are moments when their voices rise to the level of screeching. The sound of the screeching penetrates so deeply into your flesh that it almost immediately causes you to get angry. Set a limit for yourself rather than trying to endure it for as long as possible before snapping. Perhaps it will just last for five minutes. Allow them to go on for the next five minutes, then check to see whether they stop on their own. In the event that this is not the case, approach your children in a composed manner and gently shift their focus to a different game or activity.

Never, ever hit your kid. Ever.

Hitting is a short-term solution to the problem of releasing your own feelings. It does not impart any beneficial life lessons onto the youngster. It teaches kids that hitting is an appropriate response to anger, which may lead to an increase in violence inside the household or between your child and another person. The cycle of violence is a vicious one, and it's very seductive. If you strike your kid once and it made you feel better, you could feel the want to hit them again since it made you feel better the first time. If you feel the desire to beat the youngster, you should leave the room before you do so. Take some time away from the situation to compose yourself, and then come back to it when you're in a better frame of mind.

You Should Not Rely on Threats as a Teaching Method.

Threats that are made while someone is upset are often unrealistic, and as a result, it is quite improbable that you will be able to carry them out. The only way for punishments to be effective is if they are really carried out. If you do not correct this conduct, you are sending the message to your children that they can get away with it. They will then surely continue to act in the same manner, which will make you angry all over again. After then, the process continues endlessly. Instead, what you should do is come up with a series of punishments that you can fall back on and carry out. Alternately, you may tell them that you need some time to think of a suitable punishment and that you will discuss it with them at a later time. The buildup to the lesson in and of itself is educational, but you should still be sure to follow through and administer the appropriate punishment.

Keep in mind that you are the example for others to follow.

It may be difficult to accept it, but it's possible that you're contributing to the issue at hand. Your children will behave similarly to you if you have a short fuse. Your children are going to pick up life lessons from you regardless of whether or not you plan for them to. If you teach someone that expressing anger is an effective approach to cope with their feelings, then that is exactly how they will react when you do it. Be conscious of the tone of your voice as well as the words that you use while you are speaking to your children. This will assist you in dealing with your anger in a more productive manner. When you converse in a calm manner, you will feel peaceful as a result. On the other hand, the reverse is also true. You are simply going to make the situation worse for yourself if you start ranting and using curse words.

Create a list of strategies to deal with your anger when you are not currently experiencing it.

This list may be produced by both you and your children together. Both of you can learn something from this experience. The next time you find yourself becoming angry, refer to the list and choose a suitable response from among the options there. It may assist you in developing the skills necessary to channel your rage in a positive direction.

Seek the assistance of a professional.

If you find that self-help methods are not effective for you, it is perfectly acceptable to seek the assistance of a skilled expert.

The ability to keep one's cool and control one's emotions is an essential component of successful parenting. It is an unpleasant subject that the majority of parents would rather not discuss. Everybody talks about teaching kids to use the toilet and helping them with their schoolwork, but very few people admit the frustration that may come with being a parent. You shouldn't allow the fact that you're suffering prevent you from acknowledging your struggles. It is not embarrassing to put your hand up and admit that you need assistance. You are a better parent as a result of making this recognition. There is a reason why people say that it takes a village to raise a child; sometimes, experience and support are what will help you become a better communicator and parent. This is one of the reasons why people say that it takes a village to raise a child.

Causes Damage To Relationships

During our conversation on healthy anger, I made it very obvious that, if properly directed, rage has the potential to make a relationship stronger and more successful. On the other hand, destructive rage may end a relationship faster than you can blink an eye. Anger that cannot be controlled is destructive to our relationships with other people, whether they be friends, family members, loved ones, or even coworkers. In point of fact, the inability to keep one's cool under pressure is one of the most expedient ways to end a romantic connection. The effects of persistent and frequent outbursts of rage and conflicts, whether vocal or nonverbal, may be highly detrimental to the quality of our interpersonal connections. It is inevitable that you would act in an illogical and unreasonable way when you are someone who gets upset relatively often. When other people become aware of this trait in you, they will begin to maintain their distance from you, which will cause strain on your relationship. Anger, especially destructive anger, may ruin or shatter homes, families, or friendships in such a manner that it will be hard to piece the parts or fragments back together again. Negative rage may also have an effect on the relationships at your place of employment, and when there is a poor rapport amongst coworkers, the end consequence is that their efforts become ineffective.

Experiences of Annoyance and Frustration

Even though they have a lot of similarities and may seem to be the same feeling, frustration and rage are really very distinct from one another.

The emotion we experience when things does not go our way or when anything is standing in the way of us achieving what we desire is known as frustration. Because whatever a person does, no matter how hard they try, it never seems to be enough, and this may leave a person with the feeling that they should simply give up. Anger may develop when a person is unable to effectively cope with their frustration or when they grow progressively irritated by the thing that is causing them to feel frustrated in the first place.

Paranoid thoughts and feelings

Both rage and paranoia feed off of one another to amplify their respective sensations' intensity. Because anger is a reaction to a perceived danger, which may be exacerbated by paranoia, which makes a person feel as if they are being fooled in some way, misled, cheated on, or under fear of being injured, and because paranoia can make a person feel as though they are under threat of being harmed. When these two feelings are combined, they have the potential to produce a combustible cocktail that will not end well for anybody involved. This is due to the fact that both feelings tend to be a reaction to comparable triggers. It may result in heated interrogations, the individual being unable to believe whatever they are told, stalking, and emotional blackmail.

Periods of clinical depression

Sigmund Freud is credited with coining the phrase "anger turned inward" due to the fact that anger plays such a significant part in the development of melancholy. It's possible that some people found Freud's method for treating depression to be too simple; nonetheless, research seems to have backed it on more than one occasion. According to a research that was conducted in the United Kingdom in 2013, turning our anger "inward" and feeling furious with ourselves is one of the leading causes of severe depression. The majority of the topic that is covered in the research titled "The Role of Dependency and Self-Criticism in the relationship between anger and depression" is the function of anger in depression that is related with suppressed anger. When a person directs their rage inward, they often engage in high levels of self-criticism, which may result in poor levels of self-esteem as well as periods of melancholy.

Reduce Everything To Nothing

There is no better approach to cope with your anger than to get to the bottom of what's making you angry in the first place.

You've already gained some valuable insight into the true nature of the issue by doing things like thinking back on things that occurred to you in the past and figuring out where your anger came from.

Acting is the only thing left for you to do at this point. The last stage of anger management is to find a solution to the issue at hand.

This stage may bring a great deal of difficulty and difficulty, particularly if you do not know the fundamental source of the issue that you are trying to solve.

A great number of individuals experience frustration as a result of their inability to discover answers to their difficulties.

They keep making the same mistake, and it doesn't matter what they do, it seems like they always end up with the same consequences. Have you been experiencing any difficulties as of late?

Problems such as forgetting to tidy one's room, not being able to do one's assignment on time, and not being able to live up to one's standards may already cause one to feel furious inside themselves.

Getting to the bottom of these issues and finding solutions to them may effectively bring your level of rage down to zero.

In contrary to what other people believe, there are really a lot of different methods that you may cope with your anger and find solutions to the difficulties you're having.

The first thing you need to do in order to find a solution to your problem is to pinpoint precisely what the issue is. If you were unable to complete your assignment within the allotted time, then you most likely have an issue with how you schedule your time and how you prioritize your responsibilities.

Since you are now aware of the nature of the issue at hand, the following stage is formulating a strategy on how to address it. Consider the benefits and drawbacks of each approach, then choose the one that is most suited to the problem at hand.

If you have a history of putting things off until later, one of the greatest things that you can do is to develop a schedule of the tasks that you have planned for the day. This will help you stay on track and accomplish the work at hand.

And third, you should take action. Carry out your plans, and then review the outcomes of your efforts, if required. It is possible that some of your ideas may not come to fruition, in which case you will need to adjust others.

Not only can finding solutions to your issues make it easier to control your anger, but it also makes it possible for you to have a more fulfilling life.

Methods for containing and controlling one's rage

Calmness and ease

You may get better control of your anger by practicing some basic relaxation methods like deep breathing and visualization that brings about peace.

If you want to learn how to relax, there are several books and courses that can show you how, and after you have learned the methods, you will be able to utilize them anytime you feel the need to.

If you are in a relationship with someone who has a quick temper, it may be beneficial for the two of you to educate yourself on the aforementioned tactics.

You might give the following simple steps a shot:

To relax, you should focus on taking breaths that go all the way down into your abdomen rather than chest breathing, which is ineffective.

Imagine if the area you refer to as your "gut" is really where your breathing comes from.

Verbs that are known to be relaxing, such as "relax" and "take it easy," should be repeated slowly.

Repeat that to yourself while taking several long, deep breaths.

Imagery may be used to conjure up a relaxing recollection or imaginary event for you to enjoy.

Movements in the manner of yoga that are slow and simple will help you relax your muscles and feel much more at ease.

Employ these strategies on a regular basis.

Train yourself to use these strategies automatically whenever you find yourself in a stressful circumstance.

mental reorganization to take place

Changing the way you think is necessary for this, to put it more simply.

People who are angry often cuss, use profanity, or speak in a manner that is very descriptive of the intensity of their emotions.

When you're feeling unhappy, it's easy for your ideas to become exaggerated and unnecessarily dramatic.

Make an effort to come up with alternatives that are more rational.

Instead of telling yourself things like, "Oh, it's awful, it's terrible, everything's ruined," for instance, you could tell yourself things like, "It's frustrating, and it's understandable that I'm upset about it, but it's not the end of the world, and getting angry is not going to fix it anyhow."

When you're talking about yourself or another individual, try to steer clear of using phrases like "never" and "always."

Inaccurate remarks such as "This!&*%@ machine never works" or "you're always forgetting things" not only make you feel furious, but they also give you the sense that there is nothing you can do to repair the problem.

In addition to this, they embarrass and alienate others who may otherwise be eager to work together with you to find a solution to the problem.

Remind yourself that becoming upset will not enhance your mood and will not solve any problems; in fact, it may make you feel much worse.

It is impossible for reasoning to calm rage because anger, even when it is warranted, may quickly spiral out of control and become illogical.

Apply logic in order to investigate oneself.

Remind yourself that no one or object is "out to get you," and that the challenges you are facing are just part of living a normal life.

If you continue to do this every time you feel your wrath getting the best of you,

you will eventually develop a more objective point of view.

People who are angry often make demands, such as being accepted, being treated fairly, agreeing with them, and being ready to carry out their will.

We are all upset and dissatisfied when we are unable to get the things that we seek since we all have these desires. On the other hand, those who are furious want these things, and when they are not satisfied, their disappointment transforms into fury.

As part of the cognitive restructuring process, people who are furious need to learn how to transform their expectations into wants and become conscious of their own neediness.

To put it another way, it is preferable to just show an interest in something as opposed to demanding or feeling compelled to get it.

You won't experience rage, but you will feel the other common negative feelings that come along with not getting what you want, such as frustration, disappointment, and pain.

Even if some individuals who are furious utilize their anger as a coping method for injured sentiments, this does not make those feelings go away.

The Influence Of Making An Apology

The majority of people, when they have been insulted or injured by our acts or inactions, want to first and foremost be heard, but they also want an apology. The power of apology extends to repairing shattered relationships, easing the pain of wounds and wounded pride, and restoring wholeness to broken hearts. You may show the other person that you regret having wounded them by apologizing and letting them know that you are sorry. To my amazement, this has the capacity to cure even the most severe wounds. It is of equal importance that you convey to the individual that you respect him and care about the emotions he is experiencing. An apology is a method of demonstrating empathy for the person who has been harmed as well as a way of admitting an act that cannot go unrecognized without putting the relationship in jeopardy. It has the potential to calm the ire of the other person, put an end to any additional misunderstandings, and close the gap that exists between individuals. If the other person believes that you have apologized in good faith and that you are really sorry for what you have caused them, their anger may melt away or disappear completely on the moment. This is particularly important to keep in mind in the event when your behavior was unintended, such as accidentally stating something that the other person found to be hurtful to their emotions.

To briefly summarize, in order to find solutions to disputes,

Listen without taking anything personally and with an unprejudiced open heart and mind.

Try to put yourself in the other person's shoes.

Establish ground principles for the process of dispute resolution.

Make an apology to the other individual.

Dealing with People Who Have an Aggressive Anger Style: A General Prescription If you feel as if you are being assaulted by someone whose anger style is aggressive, the following coping skills will be helpful to you:

1. Regain your composure by taking several slow, deep breaths and counting to 10. Find a way to get out of there as soon as you get the sense that you could lose control of the situation. Come back when you feel like you have a better handle on things.

2. Bring Down Your Volume: People have a tendency to raise their voices when they are agitated because it makes them feel more powerful. If you respond to someone else's aggressive tone with

one of your own, the conflict is far more likely to spiral out of your control. You may assist both of you feel more at ease by just reducing the volume of your voice. This will de-escalate the issue. If you respond more quietly while the other person is speaking loudly, then the other person will need to lower their volume in order to hear what you have to say.

3. Don't take everything that's said to heart: Recognize that the other person is distressed, and that their distress may or may not be related to you in any way. You don't need to take insults or personal attacks against you, even if he or she is furious about anything you have done or left undone. You don't need to take it personally. Focus on finding a solution to the issue while making an effort to remain as distant as possible.

4. Refrain from shedding tears; doing so would lead the other person to lose respect for you and may encourage them to attack you when you are in a vulnerable state.

5. Don't raise your voice; you shouldn't do so even if the other person starts to raise theirs. Shouting won't solve anything, and it will most likely make the situation much more chaotic.

6. In the event that the other person becomes verbally or emotionally abusive or threatens physical violence, you should put a stop to the conversation and leave as quickly as you can.

Phase of sensorimotor activity

This is the first time that your kid will interact with the outside world. Even though they don't have any teeth yet, you can see that this infant is just starting to explore the environment and put its teeth into it. Children start to become aware of their surroundings while they are in the sensorimotor stage of development. Because of this, their senses play a significant part in the development of their cognitive abilities. Children would not be able to interact with the environment around them if they did not have their senses.

Take into consideration the following scenario:

At this age, children are at the point when they want to touch everything around them. They seize any opportunity that presents themselves. They are sensitive to every scent, sound, and taste. During this period, youngsters learn to explore their surroundings by using their lips. Because it takes some time for children's vision to mature to its full potential, they depend on all of their other senses to help them navigate the world. Indeed, there is something enchanted about this time. The wondrous world that surrounds children is revealed to them.

The following are the most notable aspects of this stage:

Young children are in the process of discovering movement and feeling.

Children learn to perfect fundamental skills such as gripping, gazing, hearing, and sucking as they grow.

Children become aware of the presence of things in their immediate environment.

Children are aware that they are distinct individuals from the people and things in their environment, particularly their mothers.

Children are capable of understanding the consequences of their own acts as well as the actions of others around them.

In a nutshell, this is the age when a youngster experiences everything as if it were the first time. As a result, it is essential to provide kids with as much meaningful stimulation as is reasonably feasible in their environment.

Phase before actual operations

Children enter an exciting new phase of development known as the preoperational stage when they begin to acquire the majority of their essential abilities. The ability to walk and speak are important developmental milestones. Children enter this stage when they begin to show signs of becoming more autonomous.

The following are some of the most important things that will happen at this stage:

Children quickly learn to recognize and use a wide variety of symbols to communicate their ideas, emotions, and experiences. For instance, youngsters have a tendency to link certain noises with particular things, such as the sound of a dog barking with a dog.

Children are prone to acting in an egocentric manner. At this age, children may begin to act in a self-centered manner. Additionally, they may exhibit excessive amounts of aggressive behavior.

Children primarily think in terms of the tangible. As a direct consequence of this, abstract cognition, such as the expression of feelings, remains challenging.

This is the age at which most children begin their educational careers. They are able to succeed in school because to the vast array of talents that they have previously acquired. However, children who do not fully develop their talents may have a more difficult time in the beginning stages of their schooling if they go on to face significant issues.

Concrete step of the operating process

Children's thoughts are still very much grounded in the tangible at this point. The development of logic and reasoning, on the other hand, makes it possible for youngsters to understand abstract ideas like feelings. When children are able to process their emotions, it has the effect of making them less self-centered and violent as they mature. The language and mathematical capabilities of children also make great progress during this time.

The following are the major landmarks that should be considered:

Children have developed logic and reasoning abilities that are better than adults.

Young children are able to distinguish many forms and dimensions in their environment. For instance, they are able to differentiate between tall, short, broad, and narrow attributes.

The patterns of mind that children exhibit become much more ordered.

Children start to infer generalizations by using logic and reasoning while they are young. In this setting, toddlers may learn to follow some basic norms of order and conduct, such as waiting patiently for their turn and sharing with others.

As a consequence, children grow their awareness of their own sentiments and learn to empathize with those of others. In addition, youngsters are aware of the consequences that come from their activities. As a consequence of this, kids learn to shun aggressive and self-centered conduct in favor of engaging in activities that promote sharing and community.

Adjusting Your Personal Triggers

When we speak about anger management, we are referring to the techniques that may be used to exercise control over one's emotional and physiological reactions to circumstances that trigger anger. You cannot steer clear of certain circumstances, and you also cannot steer clear of feeling furious at times; it is an inevitable emotion. You can, however, learn to manage how you respond to certain situations.

- James Seals, Indignation

To fix your triggers, you need to engage in any activity that has the goal of desensitizing your perception of your triggers, which will make you less likely to have impulsive or aggressive responses to them.

This indicates that a person is able to adopt new habits that will assist him or her in lowering the frequency with which they experience anger as a result of being provoked.

It also entails developing behaviors that override or eclipse your triggers, and as a consequence, you experience little to no anger in response to the things that would have ordinarily caused you to feel furious.

A good example of a practice that may be adopted to avoid the gradual but steady accumulation of anger is going for a walk if there is a feeling that anger is about to emerge.

After determining the cause of your frequent outbursts of anger, you will be able to ask and respond to the following questions:

How can I prevent my anger from being triggered by this action?

How can I avoid letting my temper get the best of me in this situation?

For instance, if your trigger is a rumor, some potential remedies include notifying a person in a position of authority about the incident or addressing the person who originated the rumor yourself, all the while ensuring that you don't lose control of your anger in the process.

There are a few different approaches to addressing our triggers, and they are as follows:

Do not continue to indulge the habit. That is, resist giving in to anything that can make it worse.

Put off your angry reaction for a little longer.

Acquaint yourself with the several methods of relaxation.

Eat in a Healthy Manner

Learn to deal with stressful situations in a healthy way.

Express your rage in a clear and direct manner.

Remove yourself from the person or the place that is creating your rage.

The Repercussions of Aggravated Tempers

When you start to let your anger out and take it out on other people, you'll invite a whole host of negative consequences onto yourself. Everyone avoids your company at all costs. Nobody enjoys being in the company of another person who may assault them for a little matter (and in general, exploding rage is not at all necessary), and nobody wants to be concerned about the possibility of physical conflict or any number of other issues that can crop up.

When you have a problem with this aggressive and loud rage, the first thing you will notice is that it will be very difficult for you to keep your relationships together. Everyone is included in this. Your loved ones will have a difficult time being physically near to you. They may begin to distance themselves from you and will only engage in conversation with you when they see it absolutely necessary. You could have the impression that your defenses are up and that your connection with the other person is weakening little; nevertheless, this perception will only become worse since you might feel guilty and furious about the entire scenario.

You are going to discover that your buddies do not come over as often and do not seem interested in being there. Of course not, there is no need for them to be around someone who has the potential to become violent when they get really furious. Your group of close pals will continue to narrow down until you are completely cut off from the outside world and have very few individuals in your immediate vicinity.

In addition to this, establishing a romantic connection will be quite challenging. You need to be able to keep your anger in check for a sufficient amount of time for the person to begin a relationship with you, which is not going to be easy. Even if you are able to do so, the violence, abuse, threats, and other behaviors that come along with anger are going to drive the person away.

The following difficulty will be found in your work. When you are unable to maintain your composure, it is challenging to hold down a work. Anger is a normal human emotion, and you have no need to feel guilty about expressing it. However, if it begins to get aggressive and attacks other people, and if you are unable to do your job with the degree of professionalism that is expected of you, it will be difficult for you to retain that position the way you want to. There are a lot of individuals who deal with this kind of rage, and one of the challenges they have is keeping a job, which may make them feel even less satisfied with their life.

It's possible that you'll get into legal trouble if your rage results in a significant amount of physical altercation. The police may get involved in situations involving domestic violence, bar fights, and other forms of physical abuse. It's possible that his track record may suffer, which, in the long run, will make things much more difficult.

When you vent your anger in this manner, you open yourself up to a wide variety of potential difficulties, as you can see. On the other hand, it has a tendency to be practically addicting. Because you are able to feel better and, sometimes, even enjoy the release of part of your anger, continuing to do it in this manner is almost like being addicted to a drug. When you let yourself feel angry over the tiny things, everything turns into a wonderful experience. However, by the time all is said and done, you may feel better, but no one else will feel completely satisfied.

Learning how to cope with the anger that you feel is essential if you want to make sure that you can prevent the issues that come along with it, or at the very least solve them if it's too late to avoid them. It is OK to have anger management problems; however, it is not acceptable to act on such problems in a way that causes damage to another person. If you are struggling with this form of anger issue, which is the most frequent form for males, then it is time to follow the treatment choices that we have in this book, or you may need to consult a therapist for it. If you are struggling with this kind of anger problem, then it is the most common form for men. at the store itself. Take charge.

The Languages Of Apology

So, what exactly are we going to speak about here? Where can you even begin to explain apology languages? There are a few different methods to communicate regret, and the manner in which one does so determines whether or not their apology is accepted. Listen to what I have to say about this.

Examine how your apology was received and whether or not it was accepted based on the criteria outlined below. If you find yourself in a similar situation in the future, use them to your advantage.

Language No. 1: Apologizing and Expressing Regret

The vast majority of people just say, "I'm sorry that...etc.," and then either continue talking or not. Some people will just conclude it with those three simple terms. Now, the goal is to demonstrate that you are remorseful not just of what you may have done or said, but also of what you did not do or say. This includes both actions and inactions.

I must hasten to add that another factor that goes into whether or not the apology is accepted is the manner in which it is offered. The bargain may also be sealed with effective body language. Therefore, it is important to pay attention to both the words that are uttered and the words that are not expressed.

Accepting responsibility is the second form of the language.

Saying "I was wrong" might be the phase of the process that proves to be the most difficult to complete. Some individuals will find it quite difficult to accept this fact, particularly those of us who believe that we are unbeatable and flawless in every way.

Now listen to this: there is no such thing as a flawless person, and we will all err at some point. Ensure that everyone is aware of this, and behave appropriately.

We need to accept complete responsibility for everything we do and everything we don't do. This plays a significant role in the process of our progress.

Language number three: putting things right

And now that we've cleared the first two obstacles, we're at the stage where it really starts to become fun: "How can I make it right?" Accepting the truth that things need to be done in a different way calls for humility, which is not easy to do given the difficulty of the task.

You can't keep doing the same thing over and over again and expect to get a different outcome, so you have to switch things up. This is an old saying, but it bears repeating because it's true. In the event that this problem rears its head again, you should approach one another in a spirit of humility and inquire about ways in which you may improve conditions in the time that you spend together in the future.

Language number four: upcoming adjustments

In light of this, we are making progress toward restoring the peace that was disrupted. "I will make preparations to prevent it from happening again in the future." At this point, you have expressed yourself, accepted full responsibility for your actions, and are eager to make changes. Now, you want to establish a basis for what is the ideal structure to accomplish peace in the camp.

It goes without saying that at this point, your spouse will be more likely to allow you to respect your word and demonstrate the mettle that you are made of. However, it is important to remember that this does not guarantee that they will do so. Keep in mind that this may operate in either direction, so be aware of both possibilities.

Language No. 5: Apologizing and Asking for Forgiveness

That's right, the bit about forgiving. In no way spiritual, however, in order to take the relationship to the next level of development, all parties involved need to be prepared to let go of the previous event and start the future with a clean slate. This is the only way to go on to the next level of growth.

"Are you able to locate it within your heart to..." These are the kinds of words that ought to make any burden easier to bear and open the door to fresh beginnings.

These are the most straightforward translations of the apology languages that I am able to bring to your attention. It's possible that you'll know them from your life at some point in the past. The secret is to be aware of what is going on around you, to be sensitive of what is going on, and most importantly, to respect both yourself and your spouse enough to treat each other with the compassion that you both deserve regardless of the circumstances.

Maintaining The Barest Minimum Of Temper Tantrums

The inability to control one's anger has the potential to ruin a day, a week, or perhaps a person's whole life. Helping your kid have a deeper comprehension of, and a firmer grasp on, their feelings is an important step in laying the foundation for a future in which they are emotionally stable and well-grounded.The majority of parents do not place managing their child's dissatisfaction at the top of their list of priorities for parenting. The vast majority of us did not get the message when we were kids on how to deal with frustration.Therefore, it should come as no surprise that many parents are at a loss when it comes to dealing with the issue of anger control for their children.

The process of bringing up a kid that is emotionally intelligent is a journey, not an endpoint. It is normal for you to see an increase in your child's ability to manage their emotions in one moment, and then to watch that progress fly out the door in the next. The capacity of a youngster to self-regulate will, of course, go through normal highs and lows as the child develops. The first thing a parent has to do in order to help a kid who is angry is to realize that anger is a normal feeling for children and that it is perfectly normal for their child to show it. Your youngster will want your aid in order to comprehend and appropriately deal with it.

We can only become confident and calm in the face of these small individuals with great emotions if we make place for our child's dissatisfaction and offer them the message they need to hear. It is possible to take control of one's anger and go from the passenger seat to the driver's seat when it comes to dealing with it. We will be able to assist our kid in more healthily coping with frustration if we model the behavior of working with it rather than fighting against it. If we have this structure in place, we will be able to guide young people through more tangible means of examining their anger. These are the seven most common and effective activities for managing anger that I recommend to parents to do with their toddlers.

The Most Effective Methods of Anger Management for Young People

Where exactly do you have the Tatrum located in your body?

Finding out how much of a bodily feeling wrath is is an essential step in the process of grasping it. When we are adults, almost certainly all of us are aware of the many of ways in which rage manifests itself physically for us. When I speak about this topic with children, we talk about how the body sends "rage signals." When your kid becomes more aware of the indications and signals that their body is sending them about anger, this is a clear indicator that it is time to make a course correction. To investigate this topic with your kid, all you need to do is ask them to draw a picture of their body, then ask them to color in the parts of their body where they believe fury is manifested and what they imagine it to look like. Children will often concentrate their drawing efforts on the region of the picture depicting the hands and mouth, declaring things like "rage bursts out of my hands and often throws toys!" or "anger yells out of my mouth with a thunderous voice!" while doing so. It's amazing to see how they translate their anger into a tangible shape in their actions.

A Guide To Be Used By Parents

As a parent, it is your responsibility to guide your child through this critical stage of development while they are still young. This will not only be vital for maintaining your sanity in the long term, but it will also be very significant for the kind of person your kid becomes in the future. To tell you the truth, yeah, there will be some work involved. Yes, your kid is experiencing a wide range of feelings at the moment. And sure, we are well aware of all that you are going through right now. However, it is not necessary for it to be hard in any way. There are straightforward actions you may do to help guide your kid through this stage.

Be honest about how you're really feeling. When you are feeling upset, express your frustration. Express your joy whenever you have the chance. Tell them when you feel angry and explain why. Your kid may be able to identify the feelings, but they may not have the language to express themselves. When you get into the habit of doing this, you will have solved a huge issue for yourself. What could possibly be a more effective method of instruction than showing?

Make use of visual aids to make waiting easy for yourself. This is something that we mastered after putting in a lot of work over a period of time. If you want your youngster to wait for ten minutes before the meal is ready, you should start a timer. Pointing at the clock is a surefire way to persuade your kid to get dressed quickly. Your youngster may grow more positive and realize that the wait won't last forever by using visual aids.

Instilling self-control in your kid starts with your help. Participation in many games involves taking turns at various tasks. For example, rocking a ball back and forth between your hands. Your youngster won't always be able to influence how things turn out; but, your kid will always be able to control how they respond to whatever happens to them. These sorts of games provide an excellent opportunity to teach your child an important life lesson.

Foster your child's sense of autonomy and encourage it. Allowing your kid to choose their own clothing or assisting them in pouring their own milk are also examples of activities that fall under this category. You'll be able to entrust them with additional responsibilities around the home as kids become older, such as setting the table or providing food for the animals.

Compliment your son or daughter. This is essential for the maintenance of their sense of self-worth. Make it a point to let them know when they've done a good job at something. It makes no difference whether it's something simple, like putting their toys away or swapping with a buddy, as long as they're making an effort. What is important is that you are praising their hard work and letting them know that you are pleased with their accomplishments.

When we made the decision to continue in this direction, there was a lot of research that needed to be done, and the hope that our children would have a better future kept us going. We had no idea that by making their toddler years simpler for them, not only were we making motherhood more enjoyable for ourselves, but also for our children. The purpose of gaining an awareness of how to respond to the behaviors that your kid displays is not simply to aid in their growth; at the same time, you are growing the "muscles" of your own emotional resilience. In light of this, your first instinct won't be to shout at your kid when you see them throwing a fit or sobbing so loudly that it sounds like a siren, but rather it will be to assist them go through this time like a pro!

1. Why do people become angry?

People often have a same physiological reaction when they are angry. As a result of the adrenal glands releasing hormones, the muscles in the body become stiff, the blood pressure rises, the heart rate quickens, and the pace at which one breathes increases.

Anger is a normal and fundamentally human emotion. It is often a response to a perceived or actual danger, and the intensity of the emotion may range from moderate annoyance to wrath.

In the same way that fear is connected to our need for self-preservation, so is rage. Anger, on the other hand, helps us understand when our intellectual being, our integrity, or our "self" is being attacked rather than alerting us to the possibility of being physically harmed. The presence of anger in oneself is a reliable sign that there is a problem with one's circumstances, relationships, or situations.

As a general rule, rage is assumed to originate from two different emotional states: frustration, which occurs when an individual is unable to acquire what they want, and a perception that an individual's emotions are being mistreated or ignored.

Think on it.

Typically, something will serve as the catalyst for the dissatisfaction, contempt, and disrespect that ultimately leads to rage. Do you have any ideas on what some frequent triggers for rage could be?

Please jot down your ideas in the area that has been supplied.

Your answer may either be written down or entered into a text file in the program that you use for your word processor (or in a text editor such as Notepad), and then it can be saved to your hard disk for later reading and for comparison with the alternative viewpoint that is shown in the next section.

When you are completed, click the Compare button to get knowledge about typical things that cause people to become angry.

Because anger is such a particular feeling, the things that set it off tend to be quite specific to the individual.

Betrayal, criticism, deprivation, exploitation, humiliation, manipulation, limitation, and danger are examples of common triggers that may lead to rage.

Anger may be provoked by a variety of factors, including those that are either directly or indirectly experienced. For instance, you could discover that you become furious at someone who has just mistreated you; this would be an example of a direct and external stimulus. Or, sometimes someone criticizes an idea and, despite the fact that it is not your conception, you get enraged by the criticism. This is an example of a response to an indirect, internal stimulus, and it may be a reaction to something that happened in the past, such as being branded dumb as a youngster.

A person's conduct, as well as their views, interpretations, and thoughts, may be altered by anger. In point of fact, persons who are furious are more likely to be incapable of reasonable thought. It is not difficult to see how anger might have negative impacts on the workplace given the fact that all of these aspects of communication are negatively influenced by it.

The day is not going well for Nancy. She is making an effort to maintain a cheerful attitude; nevertheless, Clarke has just asked her to take on one more responsibility that she just does not have the time for. Watch how Nancy responds aggressively to Clarke's request in the next video.

Clarke: Nancy, I was wondering if you could extract the Putnam file for me. Could you please do that for me?

Clarke asks with a cheery disposition.

Nancy: Clarke, are you serious? Are you incapable of doing anything for yourself? Nancy makes no attempt to conceal the fact that she is frustrated.

Clarke said, "Whoa, where did you get that?" Absolutely, I will take care of it personally. The astonishment on Clarke's face is replaced with assertion.

Nancy: That's great! I am limited in what I can do in this area. Disgust may be heard in Nancy's voice.

Even while Nancy's outburst was not particularly dramatic, it most likely had a detrimental effect on her relationship with Clarke. In the future, it's possible that Clarke may refrain from requesting her assistance or cooperating with her. Both the person and the business will suffer negative consequences as a result of this unfavorable conclusion.

Causes And Reasons For Anger

There are numerous different ways that individuals might conceptualize rage, but the most common ones include yelling, pointing the finger, making nasty comments, and slamming doors. These are unquestionably the behaviors of someone who is furious; yet, anger has numerous facets, and we should not confine it to a single definition. There are many other manifestations of anger that may eventually develop to fury, including but not limited to frustration, impatience, aggravation, brooding, discouragement, and releasing pent-up steam. In addition, one does not need a certain disposition in order to be classified as an angry person. People who are shy get furious, people who are cheery get angry, and people who are easygoing get angry.

It is important to keep in mind that the problem at hand is wrath, not anger. The feeling of anger is inevitable; nevertheless, it is up to us to learn how to cope with it and direct it in healthy ways. The first step in this approach is to recognize the forms that rage may take. Before we can start the healing process for anger-related problems, we need to find out what caused the anger in the first place.

A Violent and Angry World

You have to start by taking a look at the bigger picture of what's going on in the world if you want to figure out where your anger is coming from. It is necessary for you to have an understanding of how it may set off your triggers on a regular basis. Life isn't fair, and some people have it even worse as the years go by. In addition, we may get substantial amounts of anguish and irritation via the many sources of the media and the social networks. Even when we are not actively searching for it, political upheaval, violence, individuals with nasty spirits, ignorance, and disinformation are all things that we encounter. We come across both individual tragedies and natural catastrophes. Swindlers and trolls are out there with the intention of throwing us off balance by stealing our monetary gains and breaking our spirits in the process. The majority of people are inept. People have no sense of responsibility. Most people are self-centered. People are not loyal to one another and are difficult to trust. The number of channels available for communication and the dissemination of information is excessive, yet very few people seem to be able to communicate successfully. The roads and airports are both completely backed up with traffic.

Our lives are made more fraught by the presence of all of these factors. These things drive us completely insane. They bring up feelings of worry, loss, exhaustion, helplessness, fury, and rage.

To begin, it is imperative that you keep in mind that these occurrences are not taking place just to "you," but rather, they are taking place to everyone. Your life is not a personal attack on anybody else's part by the world. The world is hard for everyone, but some individuals have it far worse than you do. Despite this, some people are able to deal with the sharp jabs of life much more effectively, and as a result, their lives are filled with more possibilities via extraordinary connections, more wealth, improved health, and a great deal less suffering.

Second, in a society that is rife with division on a vast scale, it is possible that you may start to feel diminished and inconsequential, and you may even question whether or not your existence is really meaningful. Well, you most definitely do, and although you cannot and should not turn off the noise, you should find out a method to tone down the unending and oppressive bustle on the outside as well as the roar that comes from inside, both of which drive wrong judgments and push us to the point where we get angry.

Third, you are not required to bring justice to the world, despite the fact that there are occasions when we would want to. Both putting an end to the insanity and exacting retribution are beyond our capabilities. This does not mean that we do not fight for causes that are important to us. It also does not mean that we become a passive spectator of life. Nor does it mean that we allow people to take advantage of us by sitting back and doing nothing. No, this is precisely why the concept of "anger" is significant. It reveals to us that not everything is as it should be, and that there are times when we have to go against the grain in order to pursue justice; nevertheless, responding to it with outward and violent anger would simply exacerbate existing divisions, cause individuals to become more steadfast in their convictions, and produce a more difficult situation. No one will ever take a permanent stance on the side of an angry person who is filled with wrath, and no one will ever swap loyalties to join a person who is unable to control their own intense feelings.

Advice for Parents

I will present some very important suggestions that will prevent situations in which you encourage your kid's wrath, as well as some vital parenting tips, in addition to the tips that are defined for helping your child deal with anger, and I will also include some of the strategies that are outlined for helping your child deal with anger.

Stay out of fights with your parents and your siblings.

By assisting their children in developing the following particular qualities, parents may help their children avoid the usual disputes and rivalries that lead to outbursts of anger:

sacrifices of self-control and altruism in the sake of egoism

A willingness to sacrifice kindness and tenderness in exchange for intense competition

Charity and thankfulness in exchange for envy

Anger should be treated with respect and forgiveness.

A belief in God and an apathy for material things

Companionship as a remedy for isolation

The expectation of suffering

Parenting that is consistent

The chance that your child's angry outbursts will continue to occur is directly proportional to the way in which you, as the child's parent or primary caregiver, react to them. When it comes to parenting, you need to be consistent. Make sure that all of the individuals who are helping you take care of your kid have the same standards and guidelines to follow.

Your children may have a predisposition toward confusion, therefore it is important to maintain consistency in the incentives and penalties they get. It is important that you do not give in to their temper tantrums and that you remain calm and consistent regardless of where they choose to have their angry outbursts.

Show your kids that you love them no matter what, and spend some quality time with them.

When you accept your children and love them without conditions, it is much simpler for them to develop habits that are beneficial to themselves and others. They are less prone to experience feelings of frustration and anger on a regular basis.

You should make it a priority to have one-on-one time with each of your children and take part in activities with them, such as playing, going out for a snack, or reading a book to them before sleep. Because of this, you will have the opportunity to strengthen favorable relationships. In addition to this, it lays a solid foundation for the development of self-discipline and provides assistance in constructively regulating anger.

The Roots And Origins Of Angry Feelings

You not only need to acquire calming tactics that will help you deal with anger and learn how to deal with it, but you also need to learn how to suppress the emotions once they emerge in order to successfully be able to overcome feelings of wrath and to make yourself a person who is emotionally composed. In the long term, what you need is to eradicate or lessen the issue from its base, which, in turn, demands you to know why you feel excessively furious in the first place.

The study of genetics - It is well-established that irritability may be traced back to a hereditary basis. People who have an immediate family who suffers from anger issues or high blood pressure are likely to be more sensitive to these conditions themselves.

Nevertheless, even in the presence of a genetic predisposition, the existence of a strong contextual provocation is what will ultimately compel a person to act irrationally.

Family and cultural traditions – In addition to being passed down via genes, angry conduct may also be inherited from one's family by way of how it is modeled. A kid who has been brought up in a family where the parents were used to verbally and physically lashing out in rage has a greater likelihood of developing excessively aggressive behavior. This is because the child has been exposed to both types of outbursts throughout their upbringing. Some cultures, when seen in their whole, might be perceived to be more aggressive, whilst others advocate the suppression of anger and the management of it in a calm way.

Gender - Because of the close connection between gender roles and culture, there is a good likelihood that gender may influence not only the intensity of anger but also the ways in which it is expressed and how one deals with it. In the majority of societies, for instance, males are seen as being more aggressive than women, and the ways in which they lash out – mostly as a result of the social modeling they get – include verbal abuse and physical aggressiveness. On the other hand, women in certain cultures are more likely to engage in passive hostile behavior or to express more openly about how they are feeling. Although this is not true for all men or all women, the striking social features that are associated with men and women in different cultures may significantly alter the effect that rage has.

Response to circumstances - No matter what the initial issue that led to the development of wrath was, the social circumstances that triggered it nearly always were. Anger is a complicated emotion that may be caused by a number of different circumstances and the sentiments that these circumstances generate. In this context, the sensations of dissatisfaction, aggravation, pain, astonishment, and disappointment are the ones that are most usually associated with it. When one is in a difficult position and has no other means of dealing with or expressing their feelings, resorting to aggressive conduct may be a useful and frequent coping method.

It is impossible to provide a sufficient explanation for the complex phenomena that is anger by reducing it to a single classification. Many people have a variety of psychological issues that may contribute to their tendency to explode over little matters that they might otherwise dismiss with relative ease. Within the category of psychological causes, there are various sub-types, including the following:

People who are already struggling with challenges, such as poor self-esteem and feelings of worthlessness, are more sensitive to this complicated emotion. This kind of rage is driven by emotions of humiliation. Sometimes, people's personal views are triggered by the acts of others, leading them to believe that they are undesired or not good enough. It's common for people to use ridiculing the critic as a form of coping after they've been hurt by criticism. These kinds of psychological problems may be very destructive to social interactions since they often remove the capacity to absorb constructive criticism from loved ones, which can lead to the development of antagonistic attitudes.

Anger tinged with paranoia People who suffer from anxiety disorders often find themselves wondering what others are scheming against them and whether or not they are being ridiculed or insulted by others. In this scenario, any criticism is seen as a danger, and an angry response is given in order to protect oneself from what is believed to be an assault.

Anger based on moral principles is sometimes sparked by encounters with others whose worldviews are in conflict with the individual's own morals and values, and this conflict may be a source of moral frustration. When someone goes against their own convictions about what is good and bad, they may often scold them or just feel furious with them. This form of rage is caused by seeing the world from one point of view and being unable to grasp that all persons are different. This is the precise issue that needs to be addressed since it is the root of the problem.

Abuse of oneself – The individual has a tendency to assume that everything is occurring around them is their responsibility, and that if they were a better person, the scenario may not have occurred in a specific manner. This is triggered, once again, by poor self-esteem in the individual. Despite the fact that this kind of rage may not include any hostility against other people, it is often accompanied by feelings of tension, ongoing irritation, and melancholy.

Get into a schedule.

What kind of physical exercise gets your blood pumping? It does not need to be something that is really taxing on the body, such as jogging, or something that is totally absorbing, such as freehand rock climbing. If it's badminton you want to play, look into joining a team. Because they help you enhance your interactions with other people, team sports are one of the finest exercises to undertake in order to learn how to better control your anger. When you are effectively working with other individuals to achieve a common goal, you will feel less rage. You will also have an advantage at work in instances when you are required to work on group projects with other people if you do this.

Join a fitness center that provides swimming opportunities if you like this sport. You may want to try out a few various workouts before settling on the one that maintains your attention, which is an enjoyable process to go through. You will eventually discover one that you like, and gradually testing out different items, maybe with friends, can be an adventure and a stress-reliever in and of itself. Eventually, you will find one that you love.

The easiest thing is going to be trying out different workouts. The most challenging part of your new strategy will be maintaining consistency. However, if you want to be successful in controlling your anger, you absolutely have to make time for physical activity in your life. There are a few different approaches you may use to guarantee that you maintain your regimen.

First, make an effort to picture the positive changes you are bringing about in your body. In addition to lowering your risk of heart attack and stroke, improving your circulation, and relieving high blood pressure, exercise is one of the most effective ways to lower your overall stress levels. To summarize, physical activity counteracts some of the most detrimental impacts of anger and stress, which is why it is an essential component of anger management. To determine if it is helpful for you to control your anger, consider thinking of each workout as a step away from the destructive domain of your wrath. An additional advantage to your mental health is that it helps you look better and feel better about yourself, regardless of the situation.

Keep in mind that you do not need to work out on a daily basis; nonetheless, it is recommended that you do so between three and five times a week, with each session lasting between forty-five minutes and one hour. Less than this will provide you advantages, but they will be less obvious.

Especially if you do not typically schedule time for exercise throughout the day, it may be challenging to see yourself going for a run every morning if you have always detested jogging or going for an afternoon swim if you abhor the ocean. If you do not normally schedule time for exercise, it may also be challenging to imagine yourself going for a swim every afternoon. Because of this, before making a significant and life-altering decision such as this one, you need to ask yourself, "What have I enjoyed in the past?" What kinds of pursuits were included in the genuinely enjoyable recollections I have? Choosing an activity that you take pleasure in will increase the likelihood that you will continue with it over time. You won't always feel like getting up an hour earlier than normal or heading to the gym after a long day at the office. Because of this, you should do physical activity that you identify with positive emotions, as this will provide you with a little bit of additional incentive.

Not only can exercise help reduce stress, but it also offers you the satisfying feeling that you are taking care of yourself. It is common knowledge that regular physical activity is good for one's health. You will feel more confident about your physical appearance as a result of the toning and slimming effects it has on your body. Exercise also helps your sleep patterns, which may very well have been affected in the past by the stress and anger that you've been experiencing. These things have the potential to easily keep you up at night, leading you to lose sleep, sleep less deeply, and get even more stressed out. This, in turn, creates even more anger, continuing the vicious cycle and making the situation worse. But you have the power to end that cycle!

When you're done with your workout, you'll feel more at ease and tranquil. Together with intentional breathing exercises, this may help you become a physically calm person in general, which will make it simpler for you to cope with stress.

In addition to having positive effects on one's body, regular exercise is also good for one's mind. Endorphins are chemicals that are produced in the brain when you engage in physical activity. These chemicals make you feel happy. It is helpful in reducing stress. It is an effective antidepressant. When it comes to controlling one's anger, all of these things may be of tremendous assistance; but, in order to obtain these effects via exercise, time and commitment are required. If you want to see a difference, you have to put your fitness plan into action and you have to stay committed to it.

Try Your Hand at Some Meditation (Tip 10)

Meditation is one of the finest things that you can do for yourself if you want to make sure that you can keep your anger in check and take care of yourself at the same time. It does not matter whether you decide that it is a good idea to work with meditation on a daily basis to guarantee that you are keeping calm and that your anger will not bother you as much if you decide that it is a good idea to practice some meditation methods only on occasion when you feel that your anger is beginning to get the best of you, or if you decide that it is a good idea to practice some meditation techniques only on occasion when you feel that your anger is starting to get the best of you.

Meditation is a series of procedures that will allow you to release tension and will quiet down the mind so that you no longer feel irritated by some of the little things that occur on around you. These benefits will come about as a result of meditating regularly. Meditation is something that has been done for years, and it is one of the most effective strategies that you can use to keep tension at bay and to make sure that your anger does not get the better of you. You can use this approach to keep stress at bay and to make sure that your temper does not get the best of you by meditating.

You won't struggle too much to grasp the fundamentals of meditation if you give it a try. The following is a list of the procedures that you will need to do out in order to ensure that you are approaching meditation in the most effective manner:

Find yourself a calm and serene setting in which to do this. In order for you to successfully do this task, you must privacy for a period of at least fifteen minutes. Do not, under any circumstances, allow anybody to enter and disrupt what you are doing. Your bedroom or another quiet place will work just fine; just ensure that everyone is aware that they are meant to give you some space and privacy while you are doing this.

When you reach that peaceful location, it is time to settle down and make yourself at home. When possible, it is preferable to keep some decent posture by sitting on the floor with a cushion under your bottom. This is the position that is recommended the most of the time. If there is a reason why sitting on the floor is not healthy for you, the best option is to sit on a chair; nevertheless, you should make sure that your posture is great while doing so.

When you are ready, sit up straight, lay your hands on your lap, and then shut your eyes. It is time for you to make an effort to empty your mind of all thoughts to the best of your ability. During this time, you should not be thinking about the things that you need to get done, the things that are stressing you out, the things that are making you furious, or anything else.

It will be difficult at first to avoid these ideas from entering your mind, but once they do, it will become more difficult to do so. It is quite OK to take a few steps back and then slowly draw your attention back to the void. If things does not turn out as planned, you should not become angry or irritated with yourself about it. After little practice, you'll have no trouble mastering it.

It is OK for you to play some music if you find that the current level of quiet in the room is too much for you to handle. It is important that the music be gentle and calming, such as the sounds of nature or classical music, so that you may continue to have a positive mood and focus on what you are attempting to do.

You may gently get up and start the rest of your day once the fifteen minutes are over (you might want to try setting a timer so that you know when the time is up without having to check your clock or phone the entire time), but first you should take a moment to relax for a little while.

In order to get the outcomes that you want, it is recommended that you practice meditation at least once every day.

For some individuals, it might be challenging to maintain their attention solely focused on the activity at hand. We live in a world where everyone is constantly doing something, and there is always something that has to be completed. To start, all you need to do is gently draw your attention back to the work at hand, and then give it another go. Do not allow yourself to get irritated or angry because of this. Everyone will be able to progress at their own rate, and you will be able to finish it whenever it's convenient for you.

If you are finding that clearing your brain is not helping you very much, and you are becoming more and more upset as a result, it may be a good idea to give visualization a go. You will use your imagination to conjure up a picture or a scene that you would want to see materialize before you while you are meditating. Any will serve as long as it is soothing and unwinding during the whole process. Then, throughout the remaining 15 minutes of your time, you will visualize every facet of that picture, including how it appears, how things feel, how things smell, and other details. This will assist you to keep your mind focused on anything other than the anger, and it will likely also enable you to feel much more relaxed.

Everyone can benefit from meditation, regardless of whether or not they are currently struggling with stress in their life. Be careful to put some of the advice from this chapter into practice so you can see how well it can work for you.

www.ingramcontent.com/pod-product-compliance
Lightning Source LLC
Chambersburg PA
CBHW050400120526
44590CB00015B/1765